Circula
Machine
Beginners

Basic Handbook for Creative Patterns
and Stunning Designs for Newbies

Princess Jenna

Table of Content

Introduction

Circular knitting machines are critical components of the textile industry, producing a wide range of knit materials for garments, home textiles, and industrial items. These devices have been in service for over a century and have changed tremendously. In this guide, we'll look at a circular knitting machine, its work, and the types of designs available. After this guide, you'll learn more about the potential and significance of circular knitting machines in the textile industry.

The textile industry uses circular knitting machines to create knit fabrics in a continuous tubular form. These machines consist of a circular bed or cylinder with multiple needles arranged in a circle to knit yarn or thread into a fabric tube. The fabric produced by a circular knitting machine can be made with various stitch patterns, textures, and colors, making it versatile for various applications, including home textiles and clothing. Several types of circular knitting machines are available, each with unique features and capabilities. These machines have revolutionized the textile industry by increasing production efficiency and decreasing waste.

A circular knitting machine aims to make knitted materials in a continuous tubular shape. Clothing, household textiles, and industrial goods are just a few of the materials produced by these machines in the textile sector. With a circular bed or cylinder as a base, the circular knitting machine creates a cloth tube by looping yarn or thread around several needles. The stitch pattern, texture, and color may all differ in the textiles made using circular knitting machines. By improving production efficiency, cutting waste, and making seamless knitwear possible, circular knitting machines have completely transformed the textile sector. Designers and producers of textiles employ circular knitting machines to create superior, adaptable knit materials for various purposes.

Chapter One

Introduction to Circular Knitting Machine

A circular knitting machine, also known as a circular knitter, is a form of knitting machinery often used in the textile industry to make various types of knitted textiles, garments, and accessories. These machines are intended to produce seamless knitted garments noted for their comfort, flexibility, and durability. The circular knitting method employs many needles organized in a circular arrangement that work together to produce knitted fabric in a continuous loop.

How a Circular Knitting Machine Works

A circular knitting machine has multiple components, including a circular bed or cylinder, needles, sinkers, and cams. Below is a more extensive description of each part:

Circular Bed or Cylinder: This is the machine's major component, where the knitting operation occurs. It's a circular tube constructed of metal or plastic that revolves around a central axis. The cylinder is made up of many needle slits arranged in a circle.

Needles: Needles are essential for creating knit fabric by looping the yarn. They are inserted into the needle slots around the cylinder and move up and down to create the loops. Various needles are available, including latch, spring bearded, and compound needles.

Sinkers are situated below the needle slots and assist in managing the yarn's position throughout the knitting process. They force the freshly produced loops onto the needle hooks and guide the yarn through and out the needle slots.

Cams: Cams are mechanical components that regulate the movement of needles and sinkers. They are located on the machine's camshaft and are responsible for forming the knit fabric's stitch pattern.

Yarn feeders are devices that feed yarn or thread to knitting needles. Several varieties of yarn feeders are available, including positive and negative ones.

Tensioners: Tensioners control the tension of the yarn as it is passed through the machine. They

How A Circular Knitting Machine Operates

A circular knitting machine uses continuous looping to generate a knit fabric tube. Here's a step-by-step guide on how it works:

The machine's yarn feeder receives yarn from a yarn cone or creel.

The yarn is then transferred through the tensioner, which regulates the tension as it is supplied into the machine.

The needle cylinder revolves, and the machine's cams trigger the needles and sinkers, forcing them to move up and down.

The yarn is wrapped over the needle hooks and dragged down by the sinkers, resulting in a new stitch on the fabric.

As the needle cylinder revolves, the needles generate new stitches, resulting in a continuous knit fabric tube.

The stitch pattern is dictated by the design of the machine's cams, which regulate the movement of the needles and sinkers.

The knit fabric comes out of the machine in a continuous tube, ready to be cut and sewed into various garments or other textile goods.

The speed and efficiency of a circular knitting machine are determined by various factors, including the machine's design, the kind of yarn used, the stitch pattern, and the operator's expertise. Circular knitting is a highly automated method that produces vast amounts of high-quality knit fabric in a short period.

SENTRO Knitting Machines is a series of hand-knitting tool products. SENTRO series products are suitable for friends six years old and above. We'll go through the features of the Sentro Knitting Machines and show you how to cast on and off.

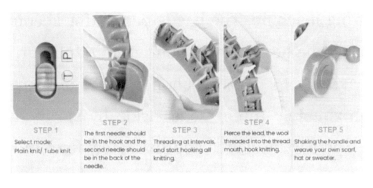

STEP 1
Select mode:
Plain knit/ Tube knit

STEP 2
The first needle should be in the hook and the second needle should be in the back of the needle.

STEP 3
Threading at intervals, and start hooking all knitting.

STEP 4
Pierce the lead, the wool threaded into the thread mouth, hook knitting.

STEP 5
Shaking the handle and weave your own scarf, hat or sweater.

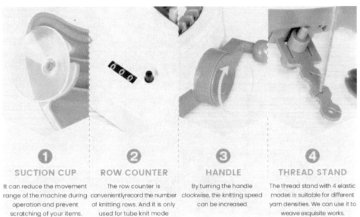

① SUCTION CUP
It can reduce the movement range of the machine during operation and prevent scratching of your items.

② ROW COUNTER
The row counter is convenientlyrecord the number of knitting rows. And it is only used for tube knit mode

③ HANDLE
By turning the handle clockwise, the knitting speed can be increased.

④ THREAD STAND
The thread stand with 4 elastic modes is suitable for different yarn densities. We can use it to weave exquisite works.

Chapter Two

How to Knit a Crossbody Phone Bag

This section will explore knitting a crossbody foam bag using the Addi Express King Size knitting machine. The bag is perfect for keeping your phone because you don't need a full purse. It's sized to fit a phone that measures approximately three inches wide by six inches tall. The bag measures approximately four and a half inches wide and a little over seven inches tall.

In timing, it takes about 15 minutes to knit the bag, 15 minutes to seam the bag, and 15 minutes to knit and attach the i-cord handle, for a total project time of approximately 45 minutes. We all go at different paces, so project time varies from person to person.

For this project, we will be using the 46-needle Addi Express King Size knitting machine, or you could also use the 48-needle sentro, and your bag will just be a touch taller. We will be using Loops and Threads Impeccable yarn, which is weight yarn and a Tulip i-cord knitter machine, but you can use any i-cord knitting machine, or you can hand-knit the i-cord with double-pointed needles. You'll also need a pair of scissors, a darning needle, a tape measure, and a knitting tag.

Step one is knitting the bag.

Cast onto a 46- or 48-needle circular knitting machine using scrap yarn. Remove the scrap yarn at the end of the project, so the colour doesn't matter as long as it contrasts well with the main colour yarn. Turn the knob until you reach the first needle. Wrap the yarn around the first needle, then weave it back and forth along all the needles until you reach the end of the row. When you approach the first needle again, wrap the yarn behind it to its right, then place it into the holder. Hold the yarn with your left hand to provide tension, or if you're using a sentro, place the yarn into the middle tensioner and begin knitting by turning the knob on the right. Knit five rows in the scrap yarn.

When you finish five rows, cut a short tail on the scrap yarn and throw it in the middle of the machine to the right of the first needle. Then, grab your main colour yarn and throw a very long yarn tail into the middle of the machine. Place the yarn tail with the scrap yarn tail between the same two needles and the yarn into the holder.

Hold the two yarn tails close together and slowly knit the next row. Pause the knitting after a few stitches to reset your counter to zero. Knit 42 rows in the main colour yarn. Knit slowly for the first few rows to ensure all the stitches are caught, and then you can pick up the speed for the remaining rows.

When you finish 42 rows, stop before the first needle. Cut another long yarn tail in the main colour yarn, which you'll use to seam the project later, and throw it in the middle of the machine. Grab the scrap yarn again and place it between the same two needles as the main colour into the yarn holder. Hold the two tails close together and slowly knit the first row of the scrap yarn cast off.

Knit five rows in the scrap yarn. Cut the scrap yarn when you finish five rows and continue knitting until the work falls off the needles. Pull the work out of the machine and gently stretch out the stitches.

Step two is grafting the ends together.

Grafting can be intimidating initially, but it's a great skill because it creates a seamless join between the cast-on and cast-off stitches. However, after some practice, it becomes a lot easier. To graft the ends together, fold up the two open sides to meet each other. Thread the yarn tail from the bottom side onto a darning needle.

Begin with the first stitch on the top right side. Go down through the first stitch and then up through the stitch directly to its left. Below is a close-up of how to work through the stitches.

Pull the yarn through. Then, go back down to the bottom side, thread down through the first stitch on the right and then up through the stitch directly to its left. Below is a close-up of the stitches being worked on. Pull the yarn through.

Next, go back to the top row. This time, you'll begin working through the stitch that you exited out of previously. Like before, go down through the stitch and then up directly to its left. Below is a close-up of working with the stitches.

Then, go back to the bottom row. Like the top side, you'll begin working through the stitch you exited out of previously. Thread down through that stitch and then up through the stitch directly to its left. Below is a close-up of the stitches being worked on.

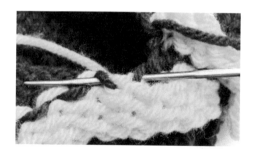

Continue in that pattern, alternating between two stitches on top, followed by two stitches on the bottom, until the end of the row. As you're working, don't pull the yarn too tightly. You're creating a new row of knit stitches, so you need the tension to match the ones above and below the grafting row. The row of grafted stitches starts to come together between the scrap yarns. Continue grafting until the end of the row.

When you reach the side of the work, flip the piece inside out and finish grafting the side, working in the same process as the other side, alternating between two stitches on the top and two stitches on the bottom.

Below is about three-quarters of the way through grafting. When you reach the last stitch, thread through every last stitch and then secure the yarn with one quick knot. We'll finalize the knot later, so just one temporary knot is great.

Step three is removing the scrap yarn.

Next, remove the scrap yarn by unwinding the yarn around the work. If it helps, you can roll the yarn into a little ball as you work or cut the yarn to shorten the tail as you unwind. One side will pull off fairly easily.

For the other side, you'll need to identify the top length of yarn running through the top layer of scrap yarn stitches. Remove the yarn a few stitches at a time for the entire first row. After removing that length, the scrap yarn should pull off much more easily.

When you remove the scrap yarn from your work, there may be a small hole at the end. If that is the case, thread the yarn onto a darning needle, stitch it up, and secure it with a knot.

Next, identify the line of grafted stitches and turn the works. That line is on the side of the bag. If the area where you started and ended the grafting has a little bump, you can turn the work inside out so the bump is on the inside of the bag. The side of the bag is now grafted.

Step four is seaming the bottom of the bag.

Thread one of the long yarn tails onto a darning needle. Use the mattress stitch to seam the bottom of the bag. To use the mattress stitch, first, look at the two pieces you'll be seaming.

Identify two lines of v-shaped stitches running in the same direction on either side. When working in the mattress stitch, you'll work through the interior bars to the side of the two rows.

Begin by threading through one interior bar on the bottom side. Pull the yarn through, thread through one interior bar on the other side and pull the yarn through.

Continue in that pattern, alternating between one interior bar on one side and one interior bar on the other side until the end of the seam. Unlike when we grafted it earlier, you can pull the yarn fairly tightly as you work, as it will create a cleaner seam. After a few stitches, you'll pull the two sides into a fairly seamless join.

Continue until the end of the row. When you reach the end, capture all the last couple of stitches and then thread the needle into the inside corner of the bag. Turn the bag inside out and secure the yarn with a few good knots. Then, thread the tail into the centre of the work to trim and hide the ends. The bag is made of a two-layer piece of knitting, so you need to hide the yarn between the two layers. The bag is almost complete.

Step five is adding a knitting tag.

This part is optional, but if you'd like to add one, attach a knitting tag to the top of your phone bag.

Step six is knitting the handles.

For this project, we will be using the Tulip i-cord knitter machine, but there are several i-cord machines on the market to use, or you can hand-knit or crochet the handle. To use the i-cord maker, thread the yarn up through the loop on the left, over the indent on the top left side of the machine, and down through the centre.

Next, add the weight to the bottom of the yarn tail. Hold the machine with your left hand, with the yarn running through a finger or two to provide tension to the yarn. With the weight pulling down, you can hold the machine in the air or place it on a table. Work very slowly at first. Turn the knob and allow the first hook to capture the yarn. Then, turn the knob, and before the second hook captures the yarn, use a crochet hook or your fingers to move the yarn behind the second needle. Turn the knob again and allow the third hook to capture the yarn. Then, turn the knob again, and before the fourth needle captures the yarn, use a crochet hook or your fingers to move the yarn behind the fourth needle. Your cast-on row is complete.

For the next row and all remaining rows, turn the knob over and allow all four hooks to capture the yarn for every row. As you work, you'll notice that the i-cord will begin to emerge from the bottom of the machine.

Continue knitting until your i-cord reaches at least 42 inches long. When knitting an i-cord, knit a little longer than you need for your pattern because removing stitches from the i-cord is easy before binding off. Measure the i-cord, and check the length you need for the handle so it's time to cast off the machine.

To cast off, cut a yarn tail in the working yarn. Rotate the knob backward for a few stitches and then forwards for a few stitches, and then the stitches will pop off the needles. Pull the i-cord out through the bottom of the machine. Before measuring the i-cord, stretch it out a few times for the most accurate measurement. Identify where 42 inches is located on your cord, pinch the i-cord at 42 inches, and then use the yarn tail to pull the stitches out until you reach your fingers gently.

Before binding off the stitches, firm up the cast-on end. The knot is already secured with the cast-on end, but the stitches can sometimes look messy. Please clean up the end by threading the yarn onto a darning needle, threading through a few stitches to pull them together, and securing that yarn with another good knot.

Next, bind off the stitches on the other side. The cast-off edge of the i-cord will have four live stitches. Thread the yarn tail onto a darning needle and thread through all four stitches, making sure to work gently so you don't pull off any stitches while you work. Pull the yarn through tightly and secure the yarn with a couple of good knots. The i-cord handle is now finished and ready to attach to the bag.

Step seven is attaching the handle to the bag.

Thread one of the yarn tails onto a darning needle and thread through three interior bars on one side of the bag. Then, thread back through the i-cord.

In the next round. Thread through five interior bars on the same side of the bag and then again through the i-cord. Continue stitching a few around the i-cord and the bag's side to ensure a strong join. Then, secure the yarn with a couple of good knots, weave it into the centre of the work, and trim the yarn to pull it into the centre. Before you attach the other side, gently untwist the i-cord if necessary. Repeat the same process on the other side of the bag, creating a strong joint between the handle and the bag. Weave in and trim the yarn tail. If you have any remaining yarn tails, weave them into the centre of the work. Your crossbody foam bag is complete.

Chapter Three

How to Knit a Mini Purse

This section will explain how to knit sweet mini purses with a circular knitting machine. The bag measures approximately five and a half by five inches for a child-size purse, and people of any age could use it. It will easily fit a phone and a small wallet. It is a pretty quick project. It takes about an hour from beginning to end: about 20 minutes knitting the pieces, 20 minutes to seam the edges, and 20 minutes to sew the pieces together. They can be customized in so many ways. You could add an initial to the front, sew on gemstones, patches, or buttons, or create duplicate stitch designs. As a reminder, if you give the purses to children or babies, you should never use buttons or any accessories that could be pulled off.

For this project, we will be using a 40-needle central knitting machine, Loops, and Threads Impeccable yarn in the colours Lavender and Lippy, a crochet hook, a darning needle, a pair of scissors, a knitting tag, and a set of small purse handles.

To begin, cast onto a 40-needle circular knitting machine using scrap yarn. Wrap your yarn around the first needle and then weave the yarn back and forth along the needles until the end of the row. When you finish the row, place your yarn into the middle tensioner. Remove the yarn at the end so the colour doesn't matter. Make sure it contrasts well with the main colour, making it easier to seam at the end. Knit five rows in the scrap yarn. When you finish the five rows, cut the tail of the scrap yarn and throw it in the middle of the machine.

Then, cut a long tail in the main colour yarn, as we'll need to use the tail later to seam up and sew the bag, and place it right next to the scrap yarn tail. Hold them close and low as you slowly knit your first row in the main colour.

Knit 75 rows in the main colour. If you want a taller bag, knit more rows; if you want a shorter bag, knit fewer rows. But the 75 is just right for the size that we wanted in this case.

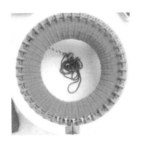

When you finish your 75th row, cut a long tail in the main colour and throw it in the middle of the machine. Then, switch back to the scrap yarn and knit five rows in the scrap yarn. When you finish the five rows, cut the tail of the scrap yarn and crank the machine until your work falls off the needles. If your work gets stuck on the last few needles, it's fine; remove them manually. Pull the work off the machine and gently stretch out the stitches. Set aside this piece for now while we knit the two side pieces.

Cast on to the 40-needle machine like you did earlier and knit five rows in the scrap yarn. Then, switch to your main colour and knit seven rows. Then, switch back to the scrap yarn and knit five more rows. Cut your yarn and crank the machine until the work falls off your needles. Gently stretch out the stitches. You can gently pull the tail yarns to tighten the two stitches when you come to the cast-off and cast-on stitch. Set the piece aside and repeat the process to make the second side of the purse. You'll now have three pieces: the main part of the bag and two side pieces.

Begin by seaming the sides of the main part. Fold the tube in half with the yarn tails to the left side. Use a crochet hook to go through the stitch to the right side, pull through the stitch directly to the left on the top side, and then pull through the stitch directly to the left on the bottom. Continue in that pattern, pulling through the next top and bottom stitch. Stitch until the end of the row. Pull the yarn tail through the last stitch and secure it with a knot when you reach the end of the row.

Next, remove the scrap yarn. Repeat the seaming process on the other side of the tube and remove the scrap yarn. We just finished seaming the main piece, and now we must seam the sides.

Follow the same process as earlier, using a crochet hook to pull through all the loops on both sides of the work and remove the scrap yarn. Repeat the seaming on the second piece as well.

Below, we have our completed pieces of the bag.

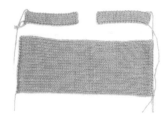

Next, sew the bag together. Grab one of the purse handles, the perfect size for the project, and wrap the top of the piece around the handle tightly. You can use a couple of stitch markers to secure the work in place as you begin to sew. Thread your yarn tail onto a darning needle, go through the first stitches on the side, and secure the yarn with a knot inside the purse. Then, sew the edge over the handle as closely as possible.

When you're stitching on the inside, you can go horizontally, but when you thread your yarn to the outside of the work, you don't want to do any horizontal stitches because you'll see them if you do. Instead, make sure you're threading your darning needle to an area between the V-shaped stitches, and then when you're threading the needle back, go over one of the interior bars before heading back to the inside. That will ensure a more seamless stitch on the outside. Continue sewing to the end of the row, finishing with a stitch through both side stitches, and then secure the yarn with a knot on the inside of the purse.

Repeat the same process on the other side of the work with the second purse handle and finish sewing the handles to the top and bottom of the purse.

Next, sew the side pieces to complete the bag. Place your side piece on the bag with the yarn tails inside the purse. Thread the long yarn tail onto a needle and go through the first two stitches several times to ensure a tight seam at the top. Secure the yarn with a knot on the inside and use the mattress stitch to sew the pieces together. Go through the seam stitches on the side piece and the bars between the side stitches on the main piece. You can either go one stitch at a time or two stitches at a time if you want to go a little quicker. When you get to the bottom, turn the corner and seam the bottom, then continue using the mattress stitch to seam up to the top. Make sure to go through the last couple of stitches a few times to ensure a tight seam, then tie a knot on the inside of the purse to secure the tail. You can leave all the yarn tails loose in the middle for now.

Next, repeat the same process on the other side of the purse with a second side piece. We're almost done with the mini purse.

To finish up, turn the bag inside out, trim the yarn tails, and secure them all with knots. Then, thread the tails onto a needle and weave in the ends. The purse is double-knit, so there will be an inside area where you can thread the needle in to leave the ends.

Turn the work right side out, and add a knitting tag. A quick reminder: if you're making the bag for a baby or children, avoid adding anything small that could be pulled off. The mini purses are complete.

Chapter Four

DIY Shoulder Purse

We will learn how to knit a mid-sized shoulder purse using a circular knitting machine. In terms of sizing, the purse measures approximately 11 inches wide by six and three-quarters inches tall, which makes it the perfect size to fit your phone, wallet, and a couple of other small items. We will go through every step of the process in this guide. We will go through how to make the bag with a zipper, but if you prefer not to sew, you can easily change the pattern to a button closure if you prefer to skip that step. There are many ways to customize the bag: knitting an i-cord for the handle, crocheting the handle, or going with a longer handle and having the bag sit closer to the hip. You could add an embellishment to the front, embellish a name, or line the inside of the bag with fabric.

For the timing, it takes about 30 minutes of knitting and about an hour to seam and assemble the bag and sew the zipper, for about an hour and 30 minutes. However, we all go at different speeds, so that the project time will vary from person to person.

The techniques we will be using include casting on and casting off a knitting machine using scrap yarn, grafting the sides of a knitting machine tube, seaming with the mattress stitch, and sewing in a zipper.

We will use a 46-needle Addi Express King Size knitting machine for the project, but you can use the sentro 48-needle machine for the pattern instead. You can follow all the same directions; your bag will end up taller. We will be using Loops and Threads Impeccable yarn in colour Cherry, and also be using a crochet hook, a darning needle, a pair of scissors, a sewing kit, pins, stitch markers, two one-inch gold rings, a purse handle, an eight-inch zipper, and a knitting tag.

Step one is knitting the bag.

To begin, cast onto your knitting machine using scrap yarn. Wrap your yarn around the first needle and then weave the yarn back and forth along all the needles until the end of the row. Then, place your yarn into the tensioner. If you're using an Addi, hold the yarn in your hand to provide tension, and if you're using a sentro, place your yarn into the middle tensioner.

Next, knit five rows in the scrap yarn. The colour of the scrap yarn doesn't matter because we'll be removing the yarn at the end of the project, but choosing a colour that contrasts well with your main colour will help when grafting the sides together.

When you finish five rows, cut a few inches long tail in the scrap yarn and throw it into the middle of the machine right before the first needle. Then, leave a long tail in the main colour and throw it in the middle of the machine next to the scrap yarn tail. Set your counter back to zero before you begin knitting. Hold the two yarn tails close and low as you slowly knit your first few stitches. Go slowly for the first couple of rows, and then you can gradually pick up the speed. Leave a long yarn tail in the main colour because we'll need to use a long tail to graft the tubes' sides and seam the bottom of the bag.

For the bag, knit 110 rows in the main colour. The number of rows you knit will determine the width of the bag, so if you prefer a longer zipper, you'll knit more rows. If you prefer a shorter zipper, you'll knit fewer rows.

A quick note about tension: tension can vary from person to person and yarn to yarn, so if you have a different tension, your piece might end up slightly longer or shorter. In a project like this, when you're fitting a particular size zipper, it's important to follow the dimensions of the pattern, not necessarily the row count.

For this bag, knit a piece approximately 10 and a half to 11 inches wide after it's grafted, giving you enough room for the rings and the zipper. Bring the knitting up inside the machine when your work touches the table.

When we finished knitting 110 rows in the main colour, we cut another long yarn tail and inserted it into the machine's middle before the first needle. Then, switch back to the scrap yarn and hold the yarn tails together closely as you slowly start knitting the scrap yarn. Knit five rows in the scrap yarn.

When finished, cut a short tail and continue knitting until the work falls off the needles. Pull the work out of the machine and gently stretch out the stitches. In this case, the final piece measures approximately 22 inches long, although it's hard to get a perfectly accurate measurement with the scrap yarn still attached.

Step two: grafting the open sides of the tubes together.

Bring the open ends of the tube together and line up the top rows of main colour stitches. Thread the bottom yarn tail onto a darning needle. Begin with a stitch directly above the yarn tail. Thread your needle down through the first stitch and then up through the stitch to the left. Pull the yarn through. Then, go back down to the stitch below, through the first stitch, and then up through the stitch to the left.

Pull your yarn through. Continue in that pattern, alternating between top and bottom stitches.

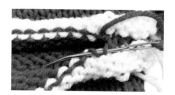 

Make sure to pull the yarn firmly but not too tightly; otherwise, your stitches will look too small. When you reach the edge, turn the work inside out and continue in the same pattern until the end of the row.

When you get to the last couple of stitches, pick up every last stitch and tie a quick knot between the two yarn tails to secure the end.

Step three is removing the scrap yarn.

Unwind the scrap yarn around the tube. One side should pull off easily. For the other side, identify the top length of yarn and pull that one length out every few stitches until the end of the row. After that length is removed, the rest of the scrap yarn should be pulled off much more easily. The final seam may be slightly visible if the stitches were grafted too tightly, but it should be barely noticeable once you move the seam to the side of the work.

Step four: seaming the bottom of the bag using the mattress stitch.

If your yarn tails aren't on the edge, thread the longer tail onto a darning needle and weave it to the bottom right corner of the bag, securing it with a quick knot. Identify the lines of V-shaped stitches running in the same direction you want to bring together. Look for the little bars directly next to those lines of stitches; these are the stitches you'll be working through as you use the mattress stitch.

Use stitch markers to help plan your work. To seam using the mattress stitch, alternate between threading through one bar on the top and one on the bottom. Repeat this back and forth until you reach the end of the row.

Remove the stitch markers as you approach them and continue seaming until the end of the row. When you reach the end, capture all the last few stitches to avoid creating holes in the corners of your work. Then, thread the yarn through to the inside corner, secure it with a few knots, and weave in the ends to the centre area of the work before trimming them. Repeat the process with the other tail, securing it with a knot and weaving in the ends. The mattress stitch should create a fairly seamless-looking join, bringing your bag together nicely.

Step 5 involves adding the rings.

If you're using circular rings, place one inside the bag and cut a length of yarn in the main colour. Thread your yarn starting from the inside of the bag, and sew back and forth one or two stitches down from the top to secure the ring in place. Ensure that the stitches you're making on the outside of the work go through the interior bars of the stitches, not over the outside stitches, for a seamless look.

Once the ring is secure, thread the needle back to the inside of the bag, secure the two yarn tails with a knot, weave in, and trim the ends. Repeat this process on the other side of the bag with the second ring.

Step 6 is optional and involves adding a knitting tag.

Step 7 is sewing in the zipper.

Use pins to keep the zipper in place, and sew it in using a thread that matches your main colour yarn. Begin under the inside of the zipper to hide the knot and sew the zipper right to the top of the work. Remove the pins as you sew, and consider using the backstitch for a stronger seam. Ensure that when sewing the outside stitches, the thread goes through the interior bars of the stitches, not over the outside stitches, for a seamless look.

Secure the thread with a knot on the inside of the bag when you reach the end of the zipper for added security.

Repeat the process by sewing a row at the bottom of the fabric. If you have extra room around the zipper, you can use your main colour yarn to add a few stitches over the zipper area.

The last step is to add your handles. You could create your handles using knitting or crocheting.

Chapter Five

How to Knit a Flower Bouquet

Using a circular knitting machine, we will learn how to knit a flower bouquet. It is a perfect springtime knitting project, and it would make a thoughtful gift for Mother's Day, Father's Day, or any other occasion where you'd send flowers to a friend or a loved one. And since you don't need to water them, they make a low-maintenance bouquet. You can also keep yours on display in your home or as a centrepiece.

We would go through every step of the process. We will be using a 48-needle sentro knitting machine, a 22-needle sentro knitting machine, Loops and Threads Impeccable yarn, a few hair elastics, some green pipe cleaners, a crochet hook, a darning needle, a pair of scissors, some stuffing, and a flower vase for this project.

Each flower comprises three parts: the outside, the centre, and the stem. In the first step, we'll learn how to knit the outside. To begin, cast onto a 48-needle knitting machine using scrap yarn. Scrap yarn is a yarn you'll remove at the end, so it doesn't matter which colour you choose. To cast on, wrap your yarn around the first needle and then weave back and forth along all the needles until you finish the end of the row. When you see your first needle again, place your yarn into the tensioner and choose the middle tension. Then, crank your machine forward to begin knitting. Knit five rows in the scrap yarn. After five rows, cut a short tail in your yarn and throw it into the machine. Then, cut a long tail in the flower colour yarn and throw it in the middle of the machine with the two tails right next to each other. You'll need a long tail, at least a few feet, to sew the flower at the end. Hold the two tails close together and low as you knit the project. Go slowly to ensure it catches all your stitches, and then you can pick up speed after a few rows.

For the flower, knit 20 rows in your main colour. After you finish 20 rows, cut another long tail in the main colour and switch back to the scrap yarn. Knit five rows in the scrap yarn. After five rows, cut a short tail on the scrap yarn and crank your machine until the work falls off the needles. If your work gets stuck on the last couple of needles, it's fine. Just pull them off manually. Gently stretch out your stitches and put the work aside while we start knitting the stem.

For the stem, follow the same procedure, casting on and knitting five rows in the scrap yarn. Then, switch to a green yarn. You don't need a super long tail for the stem. A regular-length tail is fine. Knit three rows in green, then switch back to the scrap yarn for five more rows. Cut your yarn and cast off the stitches. Gently stretch out your stitches, and when you reach the stitches where you cast them, give the green yarn tails a quick pull to tighten up those two stitches. Put your stem aside, and we'll knit the inside of the flower.

Now, switch to a 22-needle circular knitting machine. Unlike the first two parts, we won't use scrap yarn for the centre. Instead, use yellow or orange yarn and cast on directly with the main colour. Follow the same procedure, weaving the yarn back and forth along the first row, and then begin knitting. Don't count the cast-on row as a row; your first row will be the row after the cast-on. Knit 13 rows in the main colour.

When you finish 13 rows, cut a long tail in the yarn and crank the machine with some stitches.

Pull your yarn tail out from under the needle and locate the stitch from which your yarn is coming. Begin picking up stitches with a stitch directly to the left of the needle where the yarn comes out. Use a darning needle to pick up the stitch and pull the yarn through.

Continue picking them up one at a time, and then after a few stitches, you can try picking them up two or three at a time, making sure not to pull any of the other stitches off accidentally. Grab the last stitch and then gently stretch the stitches out. Pull one of the yarn tails tight to cinch one side of the work and set it aside.

It's time to assemble the flower. It would be best if you had three pieces knit: the centre, the stem, and the outside of the flower.

Begin by assembling the outside. Turn the tube inside out with the V-shaped stitches on the inside of the work. Wrap a hair elastic around the middle, just like if you were making a scrunchie. Sandwich the two sides of the scrap yarn together and line up the main colour loops on top of each other. Begin with the first stitch to the left of the cast-on yarn and use a crochet hook to pull the top loop through the bottom. Next, pull through the next top loop, then pull through the next bottom loop. Continue in that pattern, alternating between pulling through the top loop and then the bottom loop until about one and a half inches from the end of the row.

Once you're almost done with your row, stop crocheting the seam and begin to fill the flower with stuffing. You don't need to overstuff the flowers. Just a very small amount will do. Start with small amounts and push them through the tube to the bottom. Continue filling the flower lightly and evenly around the circle. Add a bit more for the area you're about to crochet, and then finish crocheting the seam. Pull the yarn tail through the last loop and secure it with a knot when you reach the end. Then, tie both main colour tails together to secure the end. Next, remove the scrap yarn. One side will likely pull off quite easily, but for the side where it's more of a challenge, identify the top yarn that runs through the loops and pull that one thread out stitch by stitch using a crochet hook or your fingers. After you remove that one yarn, the rest of the scrap yarn should pull off much more easily. We now have a little stuffed circle, almost like a doughnut.

The first step of creating the flower shape is to decide how many petals you'd like. We used five petals, and it look lovely for the flower. Your tail yarn will be where the first indent will go, so use your stitch markers to plan where the other four indents will be. To be perfect, you can count the stitches and do the math. Once you've planned where your indents will go, it's time to do the first cinch. For the flower, choose which side will be the front and which will be the back.

The back will be where we tie all the knots. We will be doing much pulling the yarn to make the flower shape, but keep in mind that as you work, you want to pull the yarn tightly but not so tight that you rip your yarn. For the first cinch, your yarn is already at the top, so use a darning needle to sew back and forth from back to front until you reach the inside of the circle. Then, pull the yarn as tight as you can without breaking it, then loop the yarn around the outside of the flower. Pull it tightly and tie a knot in a stitch in the middle to secure the cinch.

Next, thread the needle through to the inside area of the next stitch marker, tie a knot to secure the yarn, and sew in a line up to the stitch marker.

Remove the stitch marker and capture one of the top stitches, then thread the needle through the middle of the work back to the knot you tied at the bottom. Pull the yarn tightly and then wrap the yarn with one loop on the outside of the work. Pull the yarn tightly and secure it with a second knot on the inside loop. Then, thread your yarn to the next section. Continue repeating this process for all five cinches of the flower. The outside of our flower is complete. It's time to assemble the centre.

Grab your yellow project and place some stuffing in the work. Again, don't overfill with stuffing; you need a small amount. Use the yarn tail to cinch the circle closed. Use a darning needle to tie a knot to secure the opening, and then thread it through to the other side of the ball to secure the other opening. Then, tie a knot between the two tails to secure the seam. Next, push the centre through the middle of the flower and use a darning needle and the yarn tails to lightly sew the edges together so the centre doesn't fall through the flower. Next, use a needle to weave your ends through the work and trim the tails. The flower is almost done.

Next, assemble the stem. Grab your green project and flatten the work with the yarn tails to the left side. Use a crochet hook to go through the loop to the right, pull through the next loop on the top, and pull through the next loop on the bottom.

Continue in that pattern, alternating between pulling the top and bottom loop through the loop on your needle until the end of the row. Pull the yarn tail through your loop when you reach the end and secure it with a knot.

Next, turn the work over. Use a couple of pipe cleaners in the stem because it helps make them moldable and sturdy, but if you're doing this project for a child or a baby, do not use the pipe cleaner because they can have a sharp pokey end. If you choose to use them, use green because the colour will show through if the work is stretched.

Lay your work on the table with the inside facing up. Fold a couple of pipe cleaners to fit the shape of your work, and then crochet the seam closed over the pipe cleaner. Begin as we did on the other side, with the tail yarn on the left and a crochet hook to pull the loops through, starting on the right side. However, with the stem, it is easier to go from the other side of the loop and flip the stem back and forth to capture either side of the loop. Pull the yarn tail through the last loop and secure it with a knot when you reach the end. Next, remove the scrap yarn in the same way as we did with the flower.

Now, use a needle and the tail yarns from the stem to sew the stem into the center of the flower. Go through a few times to ensure it's secured tightly, then tie a knot between the tails and weave in the ends. The flower is complete.

Next, assemble all the flowers into a bouquet. Depending on how tightly you assemble the stems, some flowers might flop down when put into the vase. To make the flowers look like a bouquet, use a few lengths of yarn in the same colour as the flowers to add one or two stitches to connect the flowers. Play around with where you want each flower and continue securing the flowers to each other with a couple of quick stitches. If you'd like, you can use a bow or a piece of green yarn to tie the stems together. Next is the best part: adding the flowers to a vase.

You can use the flowers as a bouquet or knit just one flower for the vase. Play around with different colours; the possibilities are endless. If you are an avid gardener, you could even match the flower colours to the flowers in the garden.

Chapter Six

A Tote Bag

This section will cover knitting a large tote bag using a circular knitting machine. The finished tote is approximately 19 inches wide by about 22 inches tall, including the handle, and even longer when worn. The bottom area measures about 10 inches tall. We will be working on medium and extra-small sizes.

You can customize the tote in many ways. You can add a different handle, change the length of the handle, or skip the handle altogether. If you sew, consider lining the bag with fabric. This isn't a quick and easy knitting pattern, but fairly straightforward. It takes about an hour to knit each panel, totalling two hours of knitting. It takes another couple hours to seam the pieces and assemble the bag and another half-hour to knit and attach the handle. So, it takes about six hours from start to finish.

For this project, we will use a 46-needle Addi knitting machine and provide some tips on adapting this for the 48-needle Sentro. We'll use a 22-needle Addi knitting machine to knit the handle, but the machine is optional. You can prefer to use crochet or braid the handle. We will knit with Loops and Threads Impeccable yarn in the colour pumpkin and use about two and a half skeins to complete the project. We'll also use a crochet hook, a darning needle, scissors, stitch markers, and a knitting tag.

For this project, you'll need to knit two tubes of the same length. To begin, roll your machine to the first needle. Using scrap yarn, wrap your yarn around the first needle and then weave the yarn back and forth along all the needles until the end of the row. When you reach the end, place your yarn into the tensioner. If you're using an Addi machine, hold the yarn in your hand to provide tension and begin to knit. Knit at least five rows in the scrap yarn. The colour of the scrap yarn doesn't matter because you'll be removing the yarn at the end of the project, but make sure it contrasts well with the main colour, making it easier to seam at the end.

When you're ready to switch to your main colour, leave a long tail in the main colour and place it in the middle of the machine directly next to the scrap yarn tail.

Hold them close together and low as you begin to knit. Go slowly at first, and then you can pick up speed after a few rows. You must leave an extra-long tail for the project because we will use the tail to seam the pieces together and assemble the bag.

For the tote bags, knit 218 rows for each tube. If you're using a sentro 48-needle machine, we suggest knitting around 220 rows. The important part of the pattern is to match the dimensions of the final piece, not necessarily the row count. When using a knitting machine, tension can vary from person to person. For some patterns, the difference in tension doesn't make that much of a difference in the result, but your dimensions must be the same for a pattern like this.

Knit many rows; however, it takes much time to match the dimensions when working on a project. After we've seamed the pieces, if your tension and machine are similar to addi, 218 rows should work well for the project. It's crucial to knit the same number of rows for each tube. While doing the project, use a hand counter in addition to the machine counter, which gives peace of mind about the row count. If your tubes are off by one or two rows, it's not a big deal. But they won't match up properly if they're off by much more than that.

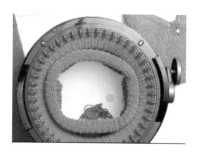

As your work gets longer and you start to touch the table, gently bring the work up inside the machine as you knit. Keep rolling the work inside as the tube becomes longer. If you run out of yarn while knitting the tube, switch to the next skein in the same way that we switched to the main colour at the beginning by placing the yarn tails together in the middle of the machine and holding them close and low as you begin to knit with the next skein.

When you finish knitting your main piece, cut another very long tail in the main colour and thread it into the middle of the machine. Then, leave a much shorter tail on the scrap yarn and knit at least five rows in the scrap yarn. When you finish, cut the tail of the scrap yarn and crank the machine until the work falls off the needles. Pull the work off the machine, unroll it, and stretch it out. You'll now have two long tubes of knitting with very long yarn tails. You can roll the yarn tails into a little ball and secure them with a stitch marker to keep things neat while you work.

The first step is to seam the edges of the tubes. Flatten your work with the yarn tails to the left side and identify the top line of the main colour loops we'll be seaming. Bring your crochet hook through the loop furthest to the right, then pull through the next loop on the top side. Next, pull through the loop on the bottom side. Continue in that pattern, alternating between top and bottom loops until the end of the row. Pull the long yarn tail through the last loop when you finish the row and secure it with a knot. Below is how your seam will look now.

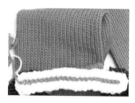

Next, remove the scrap yarn. If your scrap yarn isn't easy to pull off, identify the yarn going through the top layer of loops and use a crochet hook or your fingers to pull through the one yarn. Once you remove the length, the rest of the scrap yarn will pull off much more easily. The first seam is complete.

Next, turn the work around and repeat the same process on the other side. Then, seam both sides of the other tube. Now, we have two long, seamed tubes of knitting.

Next, seam the two tubes together using the mattress stitch. Begin by identifying the two lines of knitting you'll be seaming together and attach them temporarily using stitch markers. When knitting the mattress stitch, identify two lines of V-shaped stitches going in the same direction on either side and then work the stitch through the bars directly next to the V-shaped stitches. Those are the stitches to which we will be adding the stitch markers.

When ready to seam, thread one of the long yarn tails onto a darning needle. Start by going through the top stitch on one side to join the work. Then, thread your needle under the two bars directly next to the V-shaped stitch on the bottom side of the work.

Pull your yarn through, then thread the needle under the two bars next to the V-shaped stitch on the other side. Continue in that pattern, threading through two bars on the top, then two bars on the bottom, until the end of the row. You can also go one bar at a time if you have the patience, but the project requires much seaming, so going two rows at a time will help speed up the process a bit. As you're working, it's important to ensure you pick up stitches along the same row from beginning to end.

If you accidentally pick up stitches in the next row, it won't have the seamless look of the mattress stitch. Continue to double-check that you're working through the same line of stitches, pulling the work together. In advance, using the stitch markers will help with a lot. Remove the stitch markers as you get close to them and continue until the end of the work.

The two tubes' width is 41 inches long, and the height is approximately 13 inches tall. The goal is to match the dimensions. If you need to knit more or fewer rows than we did because your tension is different, ensure your work matches the dimensions. If you're using the 48-needle central knitting machine, your seamed tubes will likely be a touch taller, making the final piece a touch larger. So, make sure the length is a touch wider to match.

To assemble the bags, start by folding the right corner down and then the left corner up. Next, fold the right side up to the left to create a square shape with two triangles on top, forming the basic shape of the tote bag.

Then, seam the bag together using the mattress stitch, as we did earlier. Identify the lines of V-shaped stitches going in the same direction you'll bring together. Use stitch markers to bring together the stitches directly to the sides of the lines of stitches you'll be joining. Thread your long yarn tail onto a darning needle and thread it through the edge to the middle of the work.

Secure the yarn tail with a knot on the inside of the bag before you begin.

Next, go through one of the stitches on the other side to join the work. Then, work in the same process as earlier, threading the needle through two bars on the top, followed by two bars on the bottom, until the end of the row. Continue along, removing the stitch markers as you get close to them until the end of the row. Secure the yarn with a few knots, weave the ends into the bag's centre area, and trim the tail.

Flip the work over and seam the other side using the same process. When you finish, secure the yarn and weave it in the ends.

Next, add a knitting tag to your bag if desired. You can add it wherever you prefer or skip it altogether.

Now, knit the handle. Alternatively, if you prefer a much shorter handle, you could seam the top corners of the bag directly to each other and skip the step.

Using a 22-needle circular knitting machine, cast on with scrap yarn and knit at least five rows. Then, switch to the main colour and knit 100 rows for a long handle. For a shorter handle, around 50 rows may be sufficient. Switch back to the scrap yarn and knit five rows before cutting the yarn.

Seam the sides of the tube using a crochet hook in the same way as we seamed the main pieces. Next, attach the handle to the bag by seaming half of the handle edge to the right side of the corner and half to the left. Use stitch markers to keep the work in place. Secure the yarn with a knot and weave in the ends. Repeat the process on the other side of the handle.

The last step is to secure the edges where we attach the handle. That will help keep the handle tightly attached, especially when you add items to the bag. Cut a length of yarn in the main colour and use a darning needle to sew through about three to four stitches on either side of where you attach the handle. Then, tie a tight knot with the two yarn tails on the inside of the bag, secure with a couple more knots, and weave in and trim the ends. Repeat the same process on the other handle.

Chapter six

Geometric knits Bags

In this chapter, we'll learn how to knit a geometric-style handbag using a circular knitting machine. This pattern draws inspiration from the traditional granny square bag technique, often used for crochet bags. We have adapted this technique for knitting machines, giving it a bright, modern look. Throughout the section, we'll guide you through each step of the process.

The bag, when finished, should measure approximately 9 inches wide by 13 inches high, including the handle, with a bottom area of about six and a half inches high. It's designed to fit a wallet, phone, and keys perfectly.

For the timing, it takes about 45 minutes to knit the pieces, 20 minutes to seam the ends, 45 minutes to assemble the bag, and 25 minutes to knit and attach the i-cord handles, making the total project time approximately 2 hours and 15 minutes. However, project time can vary from person to person.

There are endless ways to customize the bags. You can experiment with different colour patterns, crochet, hand knit, or braid the handle instead of using the i-cord, knit the bag all in one colour, adjust the handle length for a shoulder or crossbody bag, line the inside with fabric, add embellishments, a magnetic clasp, a button closure, or knit a pocket for the inside. This section will show you how to make a multicolour bag.

We'll walk you through techniques such as casting on and off with scrap yarn, changing colours, seaming the ends, assembling the bag, using the mattress stitch for vertical and horizontal pieces, and knitting the i-cord handles with an i-cord machine.

For the project, we will be using a 22-needle Addy knitting machine. You can also use the sentro 22-needle machine. We will use the Tulip i-cord machine for the handles, but you can use any i-cord machine. You can hand knit, crochet, or braid the handle if you don't have one. We will also use the Loops and Threads Impeccable yarn in various colours. You'll also need a crochet hook, a darning needle, scissors, stitch markers, and a knitting tag.

Before we begin, knit up a sample square. The bag pattern is created using squares; your dimensions must be accurate. Tension can vary from person to person and yarn to yarn, so you may need to knit a row or two more or less. If your tension is significantly different, follow the row count. But if your squares aren't looking even, adapt the pattern so that your panels match the dimensions shown in the picture.

Step one is knitting the pieces.

The bag is created using five panels. Follow the pattern from the top to the bottom of each panel.

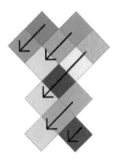

Begin with the first panel, which will be two squares. Cast onto a 22-needle machine using scrap yarn that you'll remove at the project's end. Wrap your yarn around the first needle and then weave the yarn front and back along all the needles until the end of the row. When you reach your first needle again, place your yarn into the tensioner, hold the yarn to provide tension, and turn the knob to begin knitting.

Start slowly for the first couple of rows, and then you can begin to pick up speed. Knit five rows in the scrap yarn. When you finish the five rows, cut the scrap yarn and throw it in the middle of the machine. Switch to your main colour, leaving a long tail, which we'll use to seam the headband later.

For this project, leave about a two-foot tail to be on the safe side. Leave a long tail when casting on and off for the rest of the pattern. Place the yarn tail next to the scrap yarn tail and hold it close and low as you slowly knit the next row. Set your counter back to zero.

For the first square, knit 16 rows in the first square colour

Next, switch to the second square's colour. Move the yarn colour changes off by a few stitches from the cast-on needle for the project. This is because the yarn change can sometimes create a small bump on the side of the work, making the bag seam look messy if the yarn changes occur at the same place as the cast-on stitches. So, cast on the first colour before the first needle for this bag. But when we change the colours in the middle of the panels, we purposely knit three additional needles after finishing the row count before switching to the next colour, which will move the yarn change bumps to the inside of the bag.

When you switch to the next colour, cut a tail about five or six inches long and throw it in the middle of the machine after the third needle from the cast-on needle.

Next, leave another five to six-inch tail in the next square colour and hold the two yarn tails together, close and low, as you slowly knit the next row. After you've knit a few stitches, turn your counter back to zero to begin counting the next square. Knit 16 rows for the second square.

After about five rows after each yarn colour change, tie a quick knot between the two yarn tails from the colour change. Don't double-knot it yet. Just one quick knot to secure the ends is great. We'll come back at the end to secure the knots.

When you finish 16 rows, switch back to the scrap yarn to go back to doing the switch before the first needle, just like we did when we cast on. Knit five rows in the scrap yarn. When you finish five rows, cut the yarn and continue knitting until the work falls off the needles. Pull the work out of the machine and gently stretch out the stitches. Put the work aside while we knit the second panel.

Knit the three squares for the second panel, beginning with the top square and working down to the bottom square.

Cast on again to your 22-needle machine using scrap yarn and knit five rows in the scrap yarn. Switch to your first square colour, switching before the first needle. Knit 16 rows in the first colour. When you finish 16 rows, switch to the second square colour, remembering to switch after the third needle. Knit 15 rows in the second square colour. When you finish 15 rows in the second square colour, switch to the third square colour, again switching after the third needle. Knit 16 rows in the third square colour. After you finish 16 rows, switch back to the scrap yarn, making the switch before the first needle. Knit five rows in the scrap yarn. Cut the yarn and continue knitting until the work falls off the needles. Gently stretch out the stitches and set aside the work while we knit the third panel.

Knit four squares for the third panel, starting with the top square and working down to the bottom square. It will be the longest panel.

Cast back onto the 22-needle machine using scrap yarn and knit five rows in the scrap yarn. Switch to the first square colour before the first needle. Knit 16 rows in the first square colour. After 16 rows, knit three additional stitches and switch to the second square colour, changing after the third needle. Knit 15 rows in the second square colour. Next, switch to the third square colour, again switching after the third needle. Knit 15 rows in the third square colour. Next, knit the fourth square. Switch again after the third needle to your fourth square colour. Knit 16 rows in the fourth square colour. After 16 rows, switch back to the scrap yarn. Knit five rows in the scrap yarn. Cut a short tail and continue knitting until the work falls off the needles. Gently stretch out the stitches and put the work aside while we knit the fourth panel.

Next, knit the fourth panel, which consists of three squares. Begin with the top square and work down to the bottom square.

Cast onto the 22-needle machine using scrap yarn and knit five rows in the scrap yarn. Then, switch to the first square colour before the first needle and knit 16 rows in the first square colour.

After completing the first square, switch to the second square colour, making the switch after the third needle, and knit 15 rows in the second square colour.

After the second square, switch to the third square colour, making the switch again after the third needle, and knit 16 rows in the third square colour. Once you finish the third square, switch back to the scrap yarn, switching before the first needle, and knit five rows in the scrap yarn. Cut the yarn and continue knitting until the work falls off the needles. Pull the work out of the machine and gently stretch out the stitches. Set the work aside while we knit the last panel.

Next, knit the last and smallest panel, just one square.

Cast onto the 22-needle machine using scrap yarn and knit five rows in the scrap yarn. Before the first needle, switch to the square colour yarn and knit 17 rows in the square colour. After 17 rows, switch back to the scrap yarn and knit five rows in the scrap yarn. Cut the scrap yarn and continue knitting until the work falls off the needles. Pull the work out of the machine and gently stretch out the stitches. We're done knitting, and we have five panels: the first panel has two squares, the second panel has three squares, the third panel has four squares, the fourth panel has three squares, and the fifth panel is one square.

The next step is seaming the ends. Before we seam, turn each of the first four tubes inside out so that the V-shaped stitches are on the inside and the bumpy stitches are on the outside. You'll see all the yarn tails left over from when we switched colours.

Secure all the yarn tails with knots except for the yarn tails between the scrap yarn and the cast-on and cast-off colours. As you secure them with knots, pull the tails tight enough that the stitches on the outside are brought together but not so tight that it bunches up the work. Check the outside of the work to see how your tension looks, and trim the tails.

With the tails secured and trimmed, turn the tubes right side out. Since all the tubes have open ends, use a crochet hook to seam the sides of the tubes closed. Bring the sides of the tube together, lining up the stitches on top of each other, with the two yarn tails to the left side. Arrange the stitches so that there's one stitch to the right that's perpendicular to the rest of the stitches.

Bring your crochet hook under the loop to the right, pull through the stitch to its left on the top side, and pull through the stitch to its left on the bottom. Continue in that pattern, pulling through the next stitch on the top, followed by the next stitch on the bottom, until the end of the row. Pull the yarn tail through when you reach the end of the row.

Next, remove the scrap yarn from the side that's more challenging to remove. Find the top length of yarn running through the top stitches and remove that length a few at a time. Once that length is removed, the rest of the stitches will come off more easily. Then, turn the work around and repeat the process on the other side of the panel. This process should be repeated on both sides of the remaining panels. We're ready to assemble the bag with all five panels knit and seamed.

Step three involves assembling the bag.

Place your first panel diagonally, followed by the second panel below it, with the bottom squares aligned. Add the third panel below the second one with the top squares aligned. Place the fourth panel halfway down from the third panel, then align the fifth panel with the centre square above it.

Step four is to seam the panels together.

Start with the top two panels, using stitch markers to hold them together. Thread the yarn tail onto a darning needle and use the mattress stitch to seam the panels.

Identify one line of V-shaped stitches on either side of the pieces you're seaming, ensuring they're running in the same direction. Work through the bars next to those two rows, threading through two bars on one side and then two bars on the other until the end of the row. Pull the working yarn somewhat tightly to secure the seam, but not so tightly that it bunches up. Remove the stitch markers as you approach them. When you reach the end of the row, turn the work upside down and secure the yarn tails with a few knots inside the bag to avoid them showing on the outside. Repeat this process for the remaining panels.

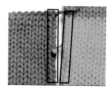 

Next, join the third panel to the second with stitch markers. Use the same process as earlier to seam the panels together with the mattress stitch.

Again, when you reach the end, turn the work over and secure the yarn with a few good knots on the back of the piece. When finished seaming the third panel, again use the mattress stitch to seam the fourth panel to the third, turning the work over to secure the knots at the end. The last step is to seam the fifth panel to the bag. Use the mattress stitch to seam the panels together, turning over the work to secure the knot at the end.

Step 5 is seaming the bag.

Place the work facing up on the inside of the bag. The back of the work will be the side with the yarn change bumps and tail knots because those are all things we need on the inside of the bag, not on the outside.

Fold the bottom half of the bag up to the top, then fold the sides in; below will be the bag's shape.

First, seam the bottom right side of the bag, then the bottom of the right square, and then the top of the right square. Then, work on the left side, seaming the bottom left side of the bag, the bottom of the left square, and the top of the square.

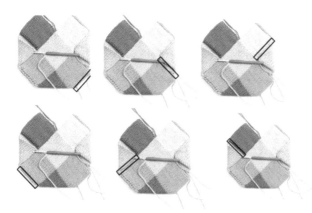

For the seams, make sure you're using a yarn tail or length of yarn the same colour as one of the squares you're seaming. When seaming the sides together, switch to threading through one stitch at a time for the side where you're continuing to pick up interior bars. Below is how to work through the V-shaped stitches for the side where you're working through the stitch.

Alternate between the two stitches until you reach the next square. As you're working, if you ever find that the sides aren't seaming equally, you can play it by ear, and if you need to work through two stitches on the bottom side to catch up to the top, that's fine.

When you reach the end of the square, switch to a colour that matches the next square. So, if your current colour doesn't match, secure the length with a knot on the inside of the bag; you can leave the tail out for now because we'll come back soon to weave in all the tails.

Cut a length of yarn in the same colour as one of the next squares and thread it onto a darning needle. Work through V-shaped stitches on both sides of the piece for the next row. Below is how to work through the stitch on the top and bottom sides.

For the side, work through one stitch at a time. For the seam, don't pull as tightly as when seaming the panels together; keep a nice, even tension as you work. After you reach the corner, you can return to the typical mattress stitch, threading through two interior bars on either side of the work, alternating between the two until the end of the row. When you reach the end, thread the yarn to the inside of the back and secure the tail with a few good knots.

Next, repeat the same process on the left side of the bag, seaming the bottom left edges followed by the two sides of the left-hand square.

Step 6 involves securing the yarn tails with knots and weaving in the ends. At this point in the project, you'll have lots of yarn tails that need to be cleaned up. Turn the bag inside out and use scissors to cut all the tails together to create a shorter length before working on them. Hiding the tails is easy with knitting machine panels because the knitting is double-layered, which means there's a centre area in each square. Thread the yarn tail onto a darning needle, thread it into the centre of the square, pull it through, cut the yarn tail close, and then wiggle the work until it's tucked into the centre. Repeat the process with all the yarn tails. Your bag is almost complete once you've finished weaving all the yarn tails.

Step 7 involves knitting the handles.

Use a Tulip i-cord knitting machine, but you can create the handles in various ways. Alternatively, you could use a crochet or braided handle. For this project, we will go through how to make the handles with the Tulip machine.

Begin by threading your yarn through the loop on the left side of the machine and down through the middle until it's coming out of the bottom. Attach the weight to the bottom of the yarn.

Hold the yarn with your left hand to provide tension, and hold the machine in the air with the weight pulled on the yarn. Make sure all four hooks are open. First, knit the setup row. Turn the knob until one hook captures the yarn, then turn it slowly for the next one. Use a crochet hook or your fingers to pull the yarn behind the second hook when you reach it. Continue turning the knob, letting the third hook pick up the yarn, and again, use the crochet hook or your finger to move the yarn behind the last hook. After the setup row, let the hooks pick up every stitch. Go slowly, ensuring each stitch is captured, and the weight pulls down through the centre yarn. After about an inch of the i-cord is knitted, increase the speed, rotating the knob until the i-cord begins to come out of the bottom of the machine.

For this project, there's no need to measure the length of the i-cord; knit until the work reaches the top of the machine. Once it's about the length, cut a six to eight-inch tail in the yarn, unloop it from the hooks, and turn the knob a few times until the work falls off the needles. Pull the piece out from the machine. Lay the i-cord out to see if you like the approximate length of the handle.

Next, repeat the same process using the machine to create the second handle. We usually make the second handle slightly longer than the first because you can always pull stitches out to make the i-cord smaller. Once both handles are fully knit, bring the first cord back to the bag and decide if you'd like to shorten it. Pinch the i-cord where you want the length to end, and gently pull the stitches out until you reach your fingers.

When you have your desired length for the first i-cord, shorten the second cord to match the first.

Again, pinch the i-cord at the desired length and pull the yarn gently to pull the stitches out.

Next, bind off the i-cords. Each i-cord will have four open loops. Thread the yarn tail onto a darning needle and thread through all four open loops. Then, as you pull the loops closed, secure the end with a knot. Repeat the same process on the end of the other handle.

Next, attach the handles to the bag. Thread one of the yarn tails onto the needle and thread through a few stitches on the top corner to ensure a secure attachment. Work that way a few times, then stitch around the edges through some individual stitches to ensure the handles are attached well. You need to make sure that it is a secure attachment.

When you're done, tie a couple of tight knots on an interior bar of the handle and weave in and trim the ends.

When you attach the other side of the handle, try to untwist the i-cord as much as possible so that the handle isn't twisted. Repeat the process of stitching the handle to the corner on the remaining three ends of the handles.

Step eight is adding a knitting tag.

This step is optional. You can add your tag wherever you prefer or place it right in the middle.

Chapter Seven

DIY Knit Pencil Cases

This section will explore knitting cute pencil cases using a circular knitting machine. The cases could be customized in so many ways. We added a pom-pom for the zipper, but you could easily swap that out for a keychain, an i-cord wristlet, or a crochet wristlet. Instead, you could decorate the cases with buttons, gemstones, patches, or other embellishments.

The pencil cases measure approximately nine inches wide by three inches tall for the sizing. If you'd like to make a taller case, you can follow the directions in the guide, but swap out the 22-needle machine for a 40-needle machine. Later in the guide, we'll explain how to adapt the pattern to be wider. The case fits about 15 pencils and pens. It would also make a great case for crochet hooks or double-pointed knitting needles.

For the timing, it takes about 12 minutes to knit the case, about 20 minutes to seam the pieces, and about 25 minutes to sew the zipper and make the pom-pom. So, about an hour in total. But everyone works at different speeds.

We will be using a 22-needle circular knitting machine, Loops and Threads Impeccable yarn in the colours jade and sunny day, a nine-inch zipper, a sewing kit, stitch markers, pins, a knitting tag, a pom-pom maker, a darning needle, and a pair of scissors.

To begin, cast onto a 22-needle circular knitting machine using a scrap yarn. Wrap your yarn around the first needle and weave the yarn back and forth along the needles until the end of the row. When you finish the row, place your yarn into the tensioner. Knit five rows in the scrap yarn. You'll be removing the yarn at the end of the project, so the colour doesn't matter as long as it contrasts well with the main colour, which will help when we seam the ends.

When you finish the five rows, cut a tail on the scrap yarn and throw it in the middle of the machine. Then, leave a long tail in the main colour yarn, at least a few feet, because we'll use the tail later to seam up the bag, and place it right next to the scrap yarn tail.

Hold them close and low as you slowly knit your first row in the main colour. For the pencil case, knit 102 rows in the main colour. The number of rows you knit will determine the width of the bag. For this case, make the zipper fit tightly and knit just enough rows to fit the zipper in. However, knit a few more rows if you prefer a little more room on the side of your zipper.

Also, note that the tension can sometimes differ from person to person. For some patterns, the difference in tension doesn't make much difference in the result. But for a pattern like this, where you're trying to match the length of a zipper, it's important to consider your tension when calculating the rows you'll be knitting.

In this instance, the goal is to end up with a piece of knitting approximately nine and a half inches wide when it's folded in half and seamed. For this, that's about 102 rows. For you, it might be a few more or a few less. For instance, if you'd like to make a longer case to hold longer knitting needles, you'd knit more rows or use a longer zipper when assembling the case.

When you finish your piece, switch back to the scrap yarn, cut a long tail in the main colour, and throw it in the middle of the machine right next to the scrap yarn tail. Knit five rows in the scrap yarn. When you finish up, cut a short tail and crank the machine until the work falls off the needles. Pull the work out of the machine and gently stretch out the stitches. Next, seam the sides of the tubes together using a technique called grafting. To graft the stitches together, line up your tubes together.

Start by seaming the top of the bottom tube to the top of the top tube. Thread your bottom yarn tail onto a darning needle. Line up the stitches directly on each other and begin with the stitch above the yarn tail. Bring your needle down through the first stitch and then up through the stitch directly to the left.

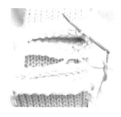

Next, go down to the bottom section of the tube and use your needle to go down through the first stitch and then up through the stitch directly to its left. Continue in that pattern, alternating between the top and bottom stitches until the end of the row. Pull the yarn through firmly but not too tight as you're working. Pulling the yarn too tightly makes the stitches look too small. As you continue, you'll see the stitches taking shape, and you can check to see how your tension looks as you work.

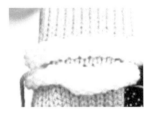

When you reach the edge, turn the work inside out to finish the other half of the seam. Below is how the seam looks before we finish the second half:

Continue until the end of the row. When you reach the end, capture all the last couple of stitches and then tie a quick knot between the two yarn tails.

Next, remove the scrap yarn. Unlike seaming one side at a time, you'll need to unwind around the work as you remove the yarn. One side will likely pull off easily. For the side that's a bit more challenging, identify the length of yarn running through the top layer of stitches and pull that length out a few stitches at a time. Once you remove that one length, the rest of the scrap yarn will pull off much more easily.

Once you've removed your scrap yarn, tie the two yarn tails together with a few knots to secure the ends. Don't trim or weave them in yet; tuck them away inside for now. The sides of our bag are now seamed. You'll see that grafting the stitches together creates a separate line of knit stitches, bringing together the work fairly seamlessly. We have the seam in the middle of the work, but we can rotate the work so that the seam is now on the edge.

The next step is to seam the bottom of the bag. Identify the two lines of V-shaped stitches that sit flat at the bottom edge. Line them up so they aren't twisted, and then use a few stitch markers to hold the work together.

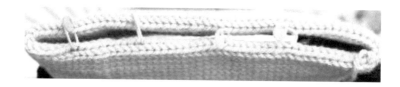

We'll be using the mattress stitch to seam the two sides together. Look for the bars inside the V-shaped stitch on the bottom and top row. We'll be alternating between those two stitches during our seam.

Thread your long yarn tail onto a darning needle and begin sewing under one of the bars on the top right side, followed by one on the bottom right. Continue until you're on the flat part, then alternating, picking up a bar on the top, followed by a bar on the bottom, until the end of the row.

As you're seaming, the work might want to twist a bit. Ensure you're watching the entire piece and double-checking that you're picking up the correct bars. Having the stitch markers in place will help with this a lot.

Continue seaming with the mattress stitch, pulling off the stitch markers as you get near them until the end of the row. When you reach the end, stitch through the last remaining hole and then thread the yarn into the inside of the bag. At this point, you can secure your yarn tails with a few solid knots and then use your darning needle to weave the ends into the inside of the work and trim the ends.

Next, add a knitting tag to the work. Normally, we add the knitting tag as the final touch, but because we'll be sewing the zipper to the top of the bag, we must add the knitting tag to the work first. You can place your tag wherever you prefer or skip this part altogether. Place it on the right side of the work with the zipper that starts on the left.

Now that the knitting tag is attached, it's time to sew the zipper. You can use a nine-inch zipper. Place your zipper on top of the bag and get a feel for where you want to sew it into the work. Use a few pins to keep the zipper in place while sewing. If you can find a thread colour that matches your work's main colour, don't worry too much if it isn't perfectly matched.

Place the thread into a regular sewing needle and bring it through to create two layers of thread. Tie a few knots at the bottom of the two threads. Begin by bringing the needle through from the part of the zipper hidden in the back. Then, push the needle through the zipper to the outside of the bag. Bring the needle under the first line of stitches, sewing as closely as you can to the zipper area so there won't be any of the fabric showing when you close your purse. When you reach your knitting tag, sew as closely as possible to the edge and then weave the thread through only the zipper fabric behind the tag. Then, start again as close to the tag as possible. Continue sewing to the end of the row. When you start to turn the corner, unzip the zipper to sew the second half onto the other side of the bag. Continue sewing until the end of the zipper. If you want an even more secure seam, sew another round of stitches along the bottom side of the zipper fabric. When you finish up, secure the thread with a knot on the underside of the zipper fabric.

The last step is to make a pom-pom. There are many ways to make a pom-pom, but we will use a pom-pom maker for this project. Wrap your yarn around one side of the pom-pom maker over and over until it's almost flat at the bottom. Cut the yarn, close it up, open the other side, and repeat the same process. Cut the yarn, close it up again, and then use a good pair of scissors to cut through all of the yarn.

Cut a length of yarn and pull it through the pom-pom maker, secure it with a knot, and gently pull the sides off. Next, pull the two halves of the pom-pom maker apart. Use scissors to trim around the pom-pom to make it nice and even.

Next, attach the pom-pom to the zipper. If your darning needle is too big to fit through the zipper hole, use the sharp part of your darning needle to push one of the tails through. Then, push the other tail through the other way. Secure the two yarn tails with a few good knots and trim the tail. The pencil case is complete.

Chapter Eight

Bow Headband

We'll cover how to make headbands in small, medium, and large sizes, along with instructions for knitting an extra-large bow. Please remember that tension can vary, so knit a sample headband to gauge sizing. You may need to adjust based on your yarn and tension.

Customization options for the headbands are endless. You can adjust the size of the bow, add embellishments, use different colours for the bow and headband, or create a two-tone bow, perfect for sports teams or gifts in school colours.

All sizes are approximately three inches tall. The small size is about eight and a half inches wide, the medium is about nine inches wide, and the large is about nine and a half inches wide.

This project is relatively quick, taking about 20 minutes to knit the pieces and 10 minutes to seam and assemble each headband, totaling about 30 minutes per headband. However, individual project times will vary.

We will get through how to cast on and off the knitting machine, seam the ends, assemble the bow, use the mattress stitch, and adjust the headband and bow size.

For the project, use an Addi 22-needle machine (or Sentro 22-needle machine), Loops and Threads Impeccable yarn in Red Hot, Arbor Rose, and Soft Rose. You'll also need a crochet hook, darning needle, tape measure, and, optionally, a knitting tag.

Step one. Knitting the main piece of the headband.

Cast onto the 22-needle machine using scrap yarn, which you'll remove at the end. Wrap your yarn around the first needle and weave it along the needles until the end of the row.

Place the yarn into the tensioner, hold it for tension, and turn the knob to start knitting. Begin slowly for the first few rows, then gradually increase speed. Knit five rows in the scrap yarn.

When you finish the five rows, cut the scrap yarn and throw it in the middle of the machine. Switch to your main colour, leaving a long tail, which we'll use to seam the headband later. Place the yarn tail next to the scrap yarn tail and hold it close and low as you slowly knit the next row. For the small headband, knit 155 rows; for the medium headband, knit 160 rows; for the large headband, knit 165 rows; and if you'd like to make the extra-large size bow, knit 170 rows. In this instance, we are knitting the size small. Remember that the headbands will stretch a bit over time, so when choosing your row count, err on the smaller rather than the larger side with your sizing.

When your work touches the table, bring it up inside the machine. If you're using a regular table, you'll need to do that a few times throughout knitting the piece. After a while, you'll need to roll the work to keep it in the centre.

When you finish your main colour row, cut a long tail in the main colour and throw it in the middle of the machine. Switch back to the scrap yarn and place the yarn tails together. Hold them close and low as you slowly knit the next row.

Knit five rows in the scrap yarn. When you finish five rows, cut a short tail on the scrap yarn and continue knitting until the work falls off the needles.

Pull the work out of the machine, gently unroll the work, and stretch out the stitches. Put the work aside for now while we knit the next piece.

Step two is knitting the centre of the bow.

Cast onto the same 22-needle machine again using scrap yarn, following the same process as earlier. Knit five rows in the scrap yarn. Switch to your main colour yarn, leaving a long yarn tail. For all sizes, knit 20 rows in the main colour yarn. After finishing the 20 rows, leave another long yarn tail and switch to the scrap yarn. Knit five rows in the scrap yarn. When you finish five rows, cut the yarn and continue knitting until the work falls off the needles. Pull the work out of the machine and gently stretch out the stitches. You'll now have two knitting pieces ready to assemble: the headband's main piece and the bow's centre.

Step three is seaming the sides of the tubes.

You'll notice that both pieces have open sides of the tubes. The next step is to use a crochet hook to seam the sides closed. Bring the sides of the tube together, lining up the stitches on top of each other with the two yarn tails to the left side. Ensure that when you arrange the stitches, there's one stitch to the right perpendicular to the rest. Bring your crochet hook under that loop to the right, pull through that stitch to its left on the top side, then pull through the stitch to its left on the bottom side.

Continue in that pattern, pulling through the next stitch on the top, followed by the next stitch on the bottom, until the end of the row. Pull the yarn tail through when you reach the end of the row; your side is now seamed. Next, remove the scrap yarn by unwinding it around and around the work. Then, repeat the same process on the other side of the work and remove the scrap yarn. For the side that's more difficult to remove, identify the top length of yarn running through the stitches and remove the length a few stitches at a time until the end of the row.

After that yarn is removed, the rest should be pulled off much more easily. Next, repeat the same process on the sides of the smaller piece to seam the sides of the centre of the bow and remove the scrap yarn from both sides. We now have two finished and seamed pieces of knitting.

For the small size, the full length of the headband before assembling is 31 and a half inches. The medium and large sizes will be longer. The centre of the bow is a little less than 4 inches long.

Step 4 is assembling the headband.

Lay the headband out horizontally. Fold one side in; the section should measure three and a half inches wide. Then, fold the other side in; the section should measure three and a half inches wide. Make the folded sections wider if you're making the extra-large size bow. Now, fold the bow sections as wide as needed to keep the headband size approximately eight to nine inches wide.

Alternatively, make the folded section smaller if you want a smaller bow. Remember that if you choose to do a smaller bow, you'll need to knit fewer rows overall so you don't end up with a headband that's too large. Then, pull both sides together.

The bow section should measure seven inches wide when the headband is folded. The headband should measure approximately eight and a half inches wide for the small size. When folded, below is how the headband will look at this point.

Next is seaming the bow to the headband. Seam together the two sides of the exterior area of the bow to the layer below them, and also seam the two headband sides together.

Step 5 is seaming the headband.

Thread one of the long yarn tails onto a darning needle. Begin by threading through one side of the bow to the back of the bow. When you place your stitches on the back of the bow, ensure you're threading over the interior bars between the stitches to create a seamless look. Make sure you're not seaming horizontally over the V-shaped stitches.

Next, thread the needle through the back of the bow to the back of the bow on the other side. Then, thread the needle back through to the top of the bow on the front. Repeat the same process, threading through the first side of the bow to the back, then threading the needle through to the back of the other side of the bow, and then back to the front. Continue in that process, pulling together all the sides until the end of the row.

As you work, make the stitches look clean on the back of the bow, but you don't need to worry too much about the stitches on top of the bow because we'll be covering that area with the centre of the bow later. When you finish the row, you'll have yarn tails on both sides of the work. At that point, use a darning needle to bring both tails to the centre of the work, then tie both yarn tails securely with a few good knots and weave in the ends. It's easy to hide your ends when working with knitting machine tubes. Just thread the yarn through a few inches into the work, trim the tail, and pull the work to bring the ends into the centre. Below is how your headband should look now: the bow sides should be attached, and the headband should be closed and wearable.

At this point, re-measure and find that the headband is still about eight and a half inches wide, and the bow is about seven inches wide.

Step 6 is assembling the centre of the bow.

To create the centre of the bow, use the mattress stitch to seam the sides to each other. Thread one yarn tail onto a darning needle and thread the needle through two interior bars on one side. Pull the yarn through, then thread the needle through two interior bars on the other side and pull the yarn through. Continue until the end of the row to create a small tube. Normally, we emphasise creating a clean seam; however, for this piece, you don't need to worry about the seam looking perfect because it will end up on the inside of the work and won't be visible. So, just a quick seam will be fine. When you finish the row, tie the yarn tails together in a few good knots to secure the ends.

Step 7 is seaming the centre of the bow around the headband.

Turn the headband inside out. Place the centre of the bow on the inside of the work with the seamed side facing towards the headband. Pull the sides together on the inside of the headband. Thread one of the yarn tails onto a darning needle to seam the sides together.

Thread the needle through both sides of one of the V-shaped stitches on the top and pull the yarn through. Then, thread the needle through both sides of one of the V-shaped stitches on the bottom side and pull the yarn through.

Pull the yarn fairly tightly as you work to create a secure seam. Continue in that pattern, alternating between top and bottom stitches until the end of the row. You'll now have two yarn tails.

Secure these tails with a few good knots, placing the knot on the side of the centre, not on the top of the centre, to avoid the headband having a knot on the side that will rest against the person's forehead. To weave in the ends, thread the yarn tails onto a darning needle and thread them horizontally across the centre of the bow, then turn around and go back the next row over. You can do that about three times and then trim the tail. Repeat this process with the second yarn tail. Turn the headband right side out.

Step 8 is adding a knitting tag.

This part is optional. For this pattern, use the skinny knitting tags because the side area is pretty small when the headbands are folded flat, but a regular-size tag will also work fine. If you prefer the bow to stay flat against the headband when worn, you can stitch it to keep it in place. Or, for the look in the photos shown earlier, you can keep it unattached. Our bow headband is complete.

Chapter Nine

Christmas Garland

Using a circular knitting machine, we will learn how to knit a simple Christmas garland. It is a fun way to decorate your home, and it's easy to customize with different colours for various holidays and occasions. In terms of supplies for this project, we would be using an Addi Express Professional 22-needle circular knitting machine, Loops, and Threads Impeccable yarn in a variety of colours, some stuffing, a pair of scissors, and a darning needle. The garland measures approximately 60 inches wide; however, the length will vary depending on your yarn and tension.

Step one is knitting the piece.

Cast onto a 22-needle circular knitting machine using your first colour yarn. Wrap the yarn around the first needle and then weave it back and forth along all the needles until you reach the end of the row. When you approach the first needle again, wrap the yarn behind the needle to its right and then place the yarn into the yarn holder. Hold the yarn with your left hand to provide tension and knit a few more stitches. Then, pause the knitting and set your counter back to zero. For the first section of the garland, knit 15 rows.

After you reach 15 rows, cut a yarn tail of about four to five inches and throw it in the middle of the machine to the right of the first needle. Then, switch to the second yarn colour by placing a tail of similar length between the same two needles and placing the new yarn into the holder. Hold the two tails together close and low as you slowly knit the next row. After a few stitches, pause the knitting and set your counter back to zero. Knit 14 rows for every remaining section except for the last section, which will be 15 rows.

After about four or five rows in the second yarn colour, pause the knitting and tie a quick temporary knot between the yarn tails. We'll come back to finalize the knots later, so one quick knot works well. Continue knitting until the second section reaches 14 rows.

Continue knitting 14 rows per section until you've reached the desired length for your garland. For reference, the garland, in this case, includes 22 sections total: 15 rows for the first and last sections and 14 rows for the 20 sections in between. As the work gets longer, you'll need to roll the work up inside the machine if your machine is set up as normal on the table.

However, if you're knitting a longer garland, you may want to set up your machine between two tables of the same height so the work falls between the tables rather than having to roll it up inside the machine.

Finishing the last section of the piece for the project will be a total of 310 rows. Now, it's time to cast off. Cut a long yarn tail and thread it onto a darning needle. Turn the knob a few stitches and identify the needle from where the yarn is emerging.

Begin with the needle to its left. Use the darning needle to pick up all the stitches off the machine, continuing to rotate the knob a few stitches as you work. After a few stitches, you can try picking up two or three at a time. Just be careful not to pull any other stitches off while you work. Pull the work out of the machine and turn the piece inside out.

Quick note: We usually prefer to use double-layered knitting for projects with stuffing because it's thicker and will hold the stuffing better over time. You also won't see through to the stuffing as much as you would with a single layer. However, using a single layer makes it easier for the project to cinch the pieces. That being said, if you prefer double-layered knitting because of the stuffing, you can achieve this in two ways. You could double the length of your knitting and bring half of the piece inside as if you were making a very long hat. Or, if that's too long of a piece to knit, you could knit two pieces in the same length and place one inside the other.

Step two is securing the yarn tails with knots.

With the piece turned inside out, you'll see many yarn tails from where you switched colours. With each pair of yarn tails, secure the yarn tails with a couple of good knots and trim the tails. Continue around the piece to ensure all the yarn tails are secured with knots, then turn the piece right side out.

Step three is adding the stuffing.

Lay the knitting out flat. Pull a handful of stuffing roughly similar to the size of one knitting section. You don't want to overstuff the work, so err on the smaller rather than the larger side so it doesn't stretch out the stitches. Place the stuffing inside the work into a section in the middle of the piece.

After you add the stuffing, gently pinch around the sides of the section. The goal is to place the stuffing in the middle of the section but not at the edges, making it easier to cinch at the end. Add a second handful of stuffing to the next section and again pinch the sides as you work to ensure the stuffing is in the centre of the section but not at the sides.

Continue adding a handful of stuffing to each section until you reach the end of the work. Pull the yarn tail to cinch the end closed after adding a handful of stuffing to the last section on one side. Secure the cinch with a few good knots. Then, using the yarn tail, tie a small loop to the end of the work, which you'll use later when displaying the garland. The first half of the work is ready.

Next, add stuffing to the other side of the work. Work in the same process, adding one handful of stuffing to each section and pinching the sides until you reach the other side of the piece. Like before, when you finish adding stuffing to the last piece, use the yarn tail to cinch the piece closed. Secure the yarn with a few good knots, and then add a loop to use when displaying the garland on the wall. You've now finished adding all the stuffing to the piece, and it's time to cinch the sections closed.

Step four is cinching the sections.

Cut a length of yarn for each section of the work. Using the length of your first yarn colour, thread the yarn onto a darning needle. Thread the yarn through the first half of each V-shaped stitch around the last row of the first section. That will create a drawstring to use when cinching. Using the two yarn tails, tie a knot as tightly as possible without breaking the yarn. Secure the knot with a second knot. Then, using the longer yarn tail, wrap the yarn around the outside of the cinch and then secure the yarn tails with another good knot, pulling as tightly as you can without breaking the yarn. Then, thread the yarn tails into the centre of the work and trim the tails.

Next, grab a length of yarn the same color as the second section and thread through the first half of every V-shaped stitch around the last row of the second section. Continue in the same process as the first section to cinch the piece. Secure with a couple of knots, wrap the yarn around a second time, pull as tightly as you can without breaking the yarn, and secure the second cinch with another couple of good knots. Weave the yarn tails into the centre of the work. You've now finished cinching around the second section of the garland. Continue in the same process, cinching every section at the last row until the end of the piece.

Your garland is complete after you've cinched all the pieces and woven in all the yarn tails. You can use the loops on the first and last pieces to attach the garland to the wall using small wall hooks.

Chapter Ten

Cat Hat

This section will explore creating a hat using the circular knitting machine. This project will use a 48-needle sentro knitting machine and Loops and Threads Impeccable yarn in black, white, and soft rose. You'll also need a heart button, sewable gemstones, a crochet hook, a darning needle, scissors, and a sewing kit.

Pull a long tail from the black yarn and place it in the middle of the machine. Set your counter to zero. Begin casting by wrapping your yarn around the first needle and weaving it back and forth across the needles until you reach the end of the row. When you reach the first needle again, bring your yarn into the tensioner and select medium tension. Knit 100 rows in black for this project.

When you knit around row 75, your work will start touching the table. Reach inside and pull the work up into the machine. Once you finish 100 rows, switch to a contrasting color as scrap yarn instead of casting off with a needle. Cut a long tail from the black yarn (a couple of feet long) and place it in the machine's center. Then, add a shorter tail for the scrap yarn. Knit at least five rows in the scrap yarn.

Cut a short tail on the scrap yarn and crank your machine for a few more rows until your work falls off the machine. Stretch out your work, and now we'll begin assembling the hat.

One half of your hat has no scrap yarn, and the other half has the scrap yarn. Use the long tail to cinch the bottom closed, pushing the work inside for a neat closure.

Moving to the top of the hat, locate the two yarn tails and keep them on the left side. Flatten the tube and use a crochet hook to go under the loop furthest to the right. Pull under the next loop on the top side and then the next loop on the bottom. Repeat this process until you reach the end of the row. Pull the yarn through the last stitch and secure it with a knot when you're at the last stitch. Then, remove the scrap yarn.

Weave the yarn through the first half of each stitch until you reach the hat's middle. Secure the yarn with a knot on the back side of the hat, right at the top. Secure the cinch side with a couple of knots, and then bring the cinch side up inside the hat to meet the flat top area. Thread the bottom tail onto a darning needle and push it through to the centre of the top to meet the top tail. Tie the two tails together. Ensure the knots are tight but not so tight that they warp the shape of the top.

To make the cat ears, cut a 12 to 24-inch piece of black yarn and thread it onto a darning needle. Use stitch markers to mark 10 stitches on each side of the corner as a guide. Sew a diagonal line from one stitch marker to the next, then thread the yarn back inside the hat and gently pull the tails to shape the cat's ear. Turn the hat inside out, tie the tails together, and weave in the ends. Repeat this process for the other ear.

To keep the brim of the hat up, use scrap yarn to add a stitch on either side of the hat, securing the brim permanently.

Sew a pink heart button onto the brim for the nose. Use a needle to push the yarn through the buttonholes and sew the button to the brim. Secure the yarn tails with a knot and weave in the ends.

Add whiskers by threading white yarn onto a darning needle and inserting it from the back of the brim to a stitch two stitches away from the button nose. Count four stitches to the right and insert the needle into the back. Secure both tails with a knot in the back of the brim and weave in the ends. Repeat the process for each whisker.

Optionally, use a sewing kit with a regular needle and thread to sew gemstones onto the ears to match a store-bought hat. Your kitten hat is now complete.

Chapter Eleven

Memo Board

This section will explore making a memo board using a circular knitting machine and an i-cord maker. This is a very simple project and a fun way to display photographs and letters. Below are the supplies we used:

- ADI Express king-size knitting machine
- weight for medium yarn
- Loops and Threads impeccable yarn in the colours C green and classic grey
- 2 skeins of sea green, 1 skein of classic grey
- 4-needle i-cord maker (such as the Tulip eye coordinator)
- Piece of cardboard at least 16 by 16 inches or several sheets of matte board in the same size (for the project, 3 sheets of 16 by 20 inch four-ply mat board were used)

- Crochet hook
- Darning needle
- Pair of scissors
- Packing tape

You can also do this project with a 48-needle sentro circular knitting machine; however, the pieces will be slightly wider, so the knitting will wrap around the cardboard differently.

The techniques you'll need to complete this project include casting on and off a knitting machine using scrap yarn, seaming the ends of a knitting machine piece, and using the mattress stitch. In terms of sizing, this project measures approximately 16.5 by 16.5 inches.

Step one is to knit the pieces.

Cast onto a 46 or 48-needle circular knitting machine using scrap yarn. Knit five rows in the scrap yarn. Switch to the main colour yarn, leaving a very long yarn tail in the main colour. Using medium tension, knit 100 rows in the main colour. Switch back to the scrap yarn, leaving a long tail in the main colour.

Knit five rows in the scrap yarn, then cut the yarn and continue knitting until the work falls off the needles. Repeat the process twice to create three pieces of the same length. Each piece has 100 rows in the main colour with five rows of scrap yarn at the beginning and end.

Step two is seaming the ends.

Use a crochet hook to seam the open ends of the work closed.

Remove the scrap yarn. Repeat the process to seam the open ends of all three pieces. You'll now have three pieces, each 100 rows, which are seamed and ready to assemble.

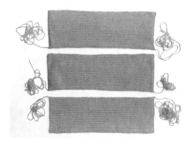

Step three is seaming the pieces together.

Use the mattress stitch to seam the pieces together. The project needs a clean seam because the seams will show on the front of the memo board. To make a clean seam, follow the same line of stitches from beginning to end.

Thread one of the long yarn tails onto a darning needle. Before seaming, look at the two pieces and identify two lines of v-shaped stitches running in the same direction you'd like to bring together using the mattress stitch. When you work the seam, thread through the interior bars to the interior sides of these lines.

Begin by threading through two interior bars on one piece, pulling the yarn through, and then threading through two interior bars on the other to pull the yarn through.

Continue back and forth between these steps; soon, you'll see a seamless join beginning to form between the two pieces. Continue seaming, following along the same line of stitches from beginning to end until you reach the other end. When you reach the end, secure the yarn with a couple of good knots. The first two pieces are now seamed together.

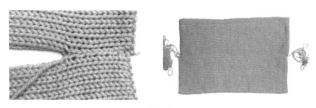

Next, repeat the same process to seam the third piece to the second. The seaming is complete, and you'll have an approximately square piece. The knitting shown below measures approximately 19.5 inches by 19.5 inches. If your piece is a little smaller or larger, that's fine.

Step four is cutting the cardboard.

After measuring your knitting, identify what size square you'd like to cut to support your memo board. A 16 by 20-inch four-ply mat board made for picture framing was used for the project. Measure out a square in your preferred size and cut out the square. The square used in this case measures 16 inches by 16 inches. If you're using thinner cardboard, you can cut out a few pieces of the same size and then tape them together using packing tape to create stronger support.

Step five is seaming the knitting around the support.

Place the knitting with the inside of the work facing up. The inside is whichever side you want hiding, and the outside is the side you want shown in the front of your board. Place the square cardboard piece over the knitting. Fold two of the sides of the knitting over the support. Give the pieces a bit of a pull so the knitting fits tightly to the support. You don't need to pull it so tightly that it stretches out the stitches too much, but you want enough tension that the knitting lays flat on the front of the memo board. Seam those sides down.

Cut a new length of yarn in the main colour and secure it with a knot on the side of the knitting. Use your preferred seaming method to seam that piece down. You can use the mattress stitch. However, the seam will not show from the front so you can use the easiest seaming method. Repeat the process on all four corners.

Next, fold the other two sides around the support, again giving them a stretch while you pull them around. Flip the piece around while placing the knitting to ensure you like the front's look. Then, seam those corners down to the knitting on the back. You can use whatever seaming method you prefer. Thread through one v-shaped stitch on one side and pull the yarn through. Then, thread through one v-shaped stitch on the other piece and pull the yarn through.

Continue back and forth, pulling tight while you work, until the piece is seamed down. Then, secure the yarn with a knot. Leave all the yarn tails free because you'll use them later. Repeat this process in all four corners of the work.

Step six is pulling the sides together in the back.

The piece of knitting will be wrapped around the cardboard support. To ensure the knitting looks tightly pulled across, thread one of the long yarn tails from the back onto a darning needle and thread through a couple of stitches across the other side. Pull the yarn firmly while you work. Go back and forth between a couple of stitches on one side and a couple on the other along the back of the knitting. The two sides are now pulled together.

Next, repeat the same process in the other direction, pulling together the top and bottom sides. You can use several different yarn tails for the process or cut a very long length of yarn in the main colour.

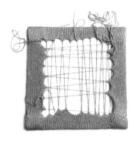

After the pieces are pulled together, check the front of the work to ensure the knitting looks how you'd like it to look. Then, turn the piece back over, trim all the yarn tails, and weave them into the centre layer of the work. The memo board is now seamed and assembled.

Step seven is adding the i-cords.

This project uses i-cords for the front of the board. If you don't have an i-cord maker, you can hand knit or crochet the i-cords instead. For this project, we will be using the Tulip Eye Coordinator. To begin, knit two i-cords long enough to wrap around the board diagonally with some extra for tying the knot. The two i-cords measure approximately 52 inches. Place the first i-cord diagonally across the front of the board. Make sure to untwist the i-cord so the stitches aren't twisted. Then, wrap the i-cord around to the back and flip the work over. Pull the i-cords tightly and tie the two ends together with a double knot. Pull the i-cord tightly to sit close to the board, which will help keep the photos in place. Turn the work back to the front and place the second i-cord diagonally in the opposite direction.

Like earlier, ensure the i-cord isn't twisted and pull the i-cord tightly while securing the double knot. You'll now have two i-cords secured in place in the shape of an X.

Next, knit four more i-cords. These can be shorter than the first two. The i-cords measure approximately 36 inches. You can leave the bind-off stitches live so you can pull out the stitches if you need them shorter. Place the board facing up and lay one of the i-cords in the position shown below, from the centre of one side to the centre of the next side. Again, flip the board over, ensure the i-cord isn't twisted, and pull tight while you tie the ends together in a double knot.

If your cast-off stitches are still alive, pull out any extra rows, secure the end of the i-cord with a knot, and weave in the yarn tails. While you're placing the four i-cords, it's fine if they don't stay perfectly still in the right spot. They should have the right tension for where you'd like them placed, with the i-cords being stretched tightly, but you'll secure them in place later in the project.

Repeat the process with the remaining three i-cords to create the memo board pattern.

Next, you may notice that the area where the i-cords should be connected to the sides is pulling apart. To bring them together, cut a new length of yarn in the same colour as the i-cords and use a darning needle to thread the yarn through both pieces. Pull as tightly as possible while securing the yarn with a couple of good knots. That will bring the two pieces together. After you've secured the two i-cords, thread through a couple of stitches on the memo board and secure with a knot, which will help keep the i-cords in place. The i-cords will now look like they're joined.

Repeat this process on the remaining three sides. You'll see that all four sides are joined together. Weave in all remaining yarn tails.

Next, cut a new length of yarn in the same colour as the i-cord and secure the corner i-cords in place to the knitting by threading through a couple of stitches in the knitting close to the back side and through the eye cord of the corner. Tie the yarn tails together tightly with a few good knots. Weave in the yarn tails. Repeat the process in the remaining three corners, which will help keep the i-cords in place.

The last step is to knit five small i-cords and bind off the stitches at about one inch long. Place the small i-cord where two i-cords meet to form an X shape. Thread one long yarn tail from right to left through a couple of stitches on the memo board, and then thread the other yarn tail back through the same stitches, going the other way. Bring the yarn tails down and then tie the yarn tails together tightly with a couple of good knots. Weave the yarn tails into the centre layer of the work. Repeat the process for all five X-shaped joints. Alternatively, you can use buttons over the areas instead.

Add a knitting tag to the side of the memo board if desired. Next, you can add photos, cards, or letters under the i-cords. Your knitting machine memo board is now complete.

To display the board, use a wall hook, such as a flat hook on the wall. You can use the yarn links running horizontally across the back of the memo board to place onto the hook or prop the board up against a wall.

Made in the USA
Columbia, SC
03 January 2025